HALFWAY HOME

by

Chaplain (Major) Felicia P. Hopkins
Veteran of Operation Iraqi Freedom

authorHOUSE®

AuthorHouse™
1663 Liberty Drive, Suite 200
Bloomington, IN 47403
www.authorhouse.com
Phone: 1-800-839-8640

*This book is a work of non-fiction. Unless otherwise noted, the author
and the publisher make no explicit guarantees as to the accuracy
of the information contained in this book and in some cases, names
of people and places have been altered to protect their privacy.*

First published by AuthorHouse   3/10/2008

ISBN: 978-1-4343-7172-0 (sc)

*Printed in the United States of America
Bloomington, Indiana*

This book is printed on acid-free paper.

Acknowledgements

Special thanks to:

Kanequa "Kace" Chancellor, Michelle Cromer, Marisol Mendoza, Kerry Jackson, Monica Garza and the wonderful people at Sanders\Wingo, Martha Gayle-Reid, Aida Smith, Charles Burkholder, my entire family and friends for their encouragement and wisdom, and all of those who served with distinction making this story possible.

Samuel, who said, "Mommy, are you still working on that book?" enough to remind me that some things take time and that persistence pays. Love you, Sammy man.

My church family at St Mark's UMC for believing in me and supporting me during my deployment, tenure and beyond.

All the brave men and women who have served with me in support of Operation Iraqi Freedom.

Last, but not least, to God, who loves all of us beyond measure and makes everything possible. For me, there is none like Him.

DEDICATED TO

The "two beats of my heart, forever
and ever ... whether near or far"

Table of Contents

Introduction

Life can be so unfair. When the bombs went off on September 11, 2001, I was almost 3000 miles away, deep in the heart of West Texas. I was dropping my children off at school and had to pull into the drive-thru lane because it was cloudy and dreary outside. I had gotten out of my car to go inside to see the nurse, Debbie, and while I was standing in the lobby, I watched the towers fall, my mouth wide open. I was saddened and horrified all at once. As I blinked my eyes, tears came rushing out of nowhere. This was not the kind of devastation I was used to seeing. It was what you saw in a movie or a third-world country, not what happened here on American soil. Instantly, I knew that this would be a day that would live forever in the minds of most adult Americans. It was just terrible, but I never imagined that this terrorist attack on American soil would turn my life, as I knew it, upside down.

I never thought I would be required to return to active duty in the Army after years of living my life quite contently as a civilian. I never thought I would go and serve in a foreign country, unaccompanied, for almost a year. I never thought I would have to share the most intimate parts of who I was with people I vaguely knew. Two hundred forty-three days after the bombing, I was ordered to go and serve in Germany, half way around the world, in support of Operation Iraqi Freedom. No one ever asked me if I would go. The decision was just made for me. I was, after all, just another reservist.

As I sit down now, a few years removed from my tour of duty, I find myself still musing over my experiences, and I am mystified that the stories I remember most somehow have come to mirror stories from my own personal life. They are stories of betrayal, abandonment, racism, friendship, service, perspective, honor, perseverance and love. When my tour of duty was up, I was just happy to be home. Then people began to ask me about the war and what I saw and what I felt helping our wounded troops. This book is a collection of a few of my experiences in the war, as seen through the autobiographical lens of my own life. I did not want to write a scathing memoir, nor one where my memories were soured by the political climate that led us into war and has ultimately caused us to lose thousands of valuable lives. I believe that God has a purpose and a reason for everything that we experience — even this war. Through my service as a Chaplain, I was privileged to serve with and give service to some of the most amazing people in my life. I dedicate this book to all who have served, because "all gave some and some gave all."

Fear

"Fear not, for I am with thee ..."

In 2003, hundreds of thousands of reservists were ordered to active duty in support of Operation Iraqi Freedom. The call-up was historical to say the least and the timing unforgiving. When I was called, I was very busy with my life. I was a civilian working as the Director for the Campus Ministry Program at the University of Texas at El Paso — a commuter college in West Texas. I was also a worship consultant for a midsize United Methodist Church. Most importantly, I was a loving, doting mother for two young boys, ages 5 and 7. Adam, my youngest, had just been through surgery six months earlier to remove a tumor near his brain, and Samuel was in second grade, struggling with reading and the need to fit in.

Yes, I was an active reservist, an Army chaplain assigned to a U.S. Reserve Army hospital. I was participating in my monthly drills. But, the truth is — I NEVER thought I would be called up to actually go to a war zone. My assigned unit's war mission was to backfill a local Army hospital 12 miles from my home — exactly why I joined the unit to start with.

So when I received a call telling me to pack two duffel bags and report to a *different* unit for deployment overseas, I was shocked, horrified, and more afraid than I had ever been. What did they mean the country was going to war and I was now scheduled to go to Germany? I remember exactly where I was when it really hit me — sitting in my car in the parking lot of William Beaumont Army Medical Center. Shaking, I gripped my steering wheel and decided that if this was true, I would need one good cry and a plan to survive.

In less than 48 hours, I was to be plucked away from everything that was familiar to me — my home, my church, and my family and friends. All I could think was "Who is going to take care of my children?" Who would preach at my church? Who would work at the college? How long would I really be gone? Where would I stay? Fear gripped me in an unusual way. It had me hostage and I felt as though I could not move. I had not felt this defeated in over 25 years. I was clearly afraid of going to war and of what awaited me overseas. Sure, I had been a hospital chaplain before, but I knew this would be different. I wanted to run and hide. I wanted to just say "No." I wanted this all to be a dream. But, that was not the case. I read somewhere that "courage is being able to do the harder right over the easier wrong." I knew deep inside that I needed to be strong and to cast my fear aside, so I said a prayer.

After being notified, I reached for my cell phone and called my mom. I sobbed until I could compose myself and ask her if she could come and help. I wanted her to "watch" my boys. *Watch them*, as though I were going on vacation and would soon return with pictures or souvenirs. I could hear my mom crying, too, breathing silently on the other end; then I heard her say, "Whatever you need, I will be there." Eight hours after my call, my mom boarded a red-eye flight out of Buffalo, New York, with one bag full of clothes she could just wash repeatedly until my return.

I can't really put into words what happened in the next 40 hours. I called my husband to tell him the bad news. He was away on business in Phoenix, Arizona, and would not return in time to see me off. I made an appointment with a friend's lawyer to create a will. I found an accountant to file my taxes. I got my car serviced, went grocery shopping, and tore up my garage looking for the required Army gear to pack and take in my mandated two duffel bags and a carry-on. I also sat down late Saturday night and wrote a farewell sermon for my congregation about being strong in the face of adversity. A sermon I had never preached before about a brave, ordinary woman named Rizpah.

But in all I did, I still had to sit down with my two boys and explain to them what was going on. As best I could, I tried to think of what I could say at a time like this. I took a long, deep breath and gathered my boys next to me in the living room on our black leather sofa. I pulled them in for a group hug and explained that, years ago, I made a promise to the Army that if there was ever a crisis or war, and they needed me to help soldiers who would be fighting to defend our right to freedom, I would go. In my best mommy voice, I said, "A promise is a promise," and once made, it could not be forsaken. Tears slowly falling out of the corners of my eyes, I concluded that maybe God created me for such a time as this. I held them tightly as if there would be no tomorrow, and then with all the strength I could muster, I picked up my duffel bags, hugged my mom goodbye, and walked right out my front door — very afraid.

Fear is real when you feel it. It doesn't matter what anyone else says or does, there will be moments when we will be paralyzed by fear. Leaving my house, I was paralyzed. I had no idea what awaited me. I did not know the unit or the people or the town I was going to. All I knew was that I was not alone. My faith was struggling for room. I realized quickly that when you begin to operate in fear, you cast out your faith. How many times had I told my congregation not to be afraid, that God was always with us, in us, and voting for our success? I knew I had to make a choice. So I decided to *DO IT AFRAID*. I decided to be like Jesus' disciple Peter and just take a step into the unknown, trusting that if I would make one step in this voyage, that God would make two. I reminded myself that fear would not operate in me as long as I kept God in my heart and on my mind. After all, I was going to be *the* chaplain. I turned and looked momentarily at my front door, vowing not to walk in fear, but in faith, until I returned. I gave the two people I loved most in that moment to the one who loved me more.

Hope

"Keep Hope Alive"

I had been stationed in Germany during the '80s. I wasn't a chaplain then, but a young, eager military police officer. As I awaited my flight back to Germany, I began to reminisce about how beautiful the countryside would be. I remembered a quiet, peaceful springtime in Germany. If it was as I remembered, everything would be green and lush. There would be rolling mountains; big, wide, drooping trees; and miles and miles of fertile vineyards lining the autobahn with ready-to-harvest grapes, lush and sweet. I closed my eyes and thought of trips to exotic places like Paris, Italy and Switzerland.

Clearly, I had fond memories of being in Germany. I had served there for three years but had never been to Landstuhl. I knew it was in close proximity to Ramstein Air Base, in the center of Germany, about 100 miles from the French border. A friend's dad, who had worked there in 1986, told me that Landstuhl was your typical picturesque small German town, with narrow, cobbled streets lined with flower shops and historic castles. He said that the hospital was situated on top of a hill on the outskirts of town, and you had to drive up a long, winding, narrow road to get to it. It was, he thought, still fully equipped to serve the needs of "America's sons and daughters abroad."

We arrived in Germany after a tense 12-hour flight on a chartered American plane. There was dew on the ground and a crisp freshness to the morning air. The war in Iraq had begun that night, as we were flying over the Atlantic Ocean. When the doors of the aircraft were flung open, the commander of Landstuhl Regional Medical Center (LRMC), and a host of soldiers and airmen already stationed there, greeted us. They were *soooo* happy to see us. They had been tackling all of the casualties for the past 18 months from Africa, Afghanistan, Bosnia and every other place in the region. These troops were worn out, physically and mentally, and had no idea how they would continue to treat the estimated extra 150 patients a day from Iraq that had just been projected.

After a few snacks and a short speech, we loaded some blue Air Force school buses for the short trip to LRMC. I was quickly assigned to a condemned, old, brick, four-story, three-bedroom, one-bath vacant apartment to share with eight other women. I was not happy, but I knew instantly that it was better than living in a tent — *been there, done that!* I dropped my bags, claimed a bunk, and, not needing to worry about decorating, made my way the half mile over to the hospital to see what *exactly* I had come all this way for.

Don't get me wrong — I knew what hospital chaplains did. I had one unit of Clinical Pastoral Education (CPE). But, I couldn't imagine that I had flown thousands of miles with a heightened sense of urgency just to do room visits and pray quietly over the sick. As I walked the seemingly empty halls of the hospital, I began to question God — "What on earth did you bring *me* here for?" I thought, "This place is pretty vacant. Where are all the injured soldiers?"

It would take me just one more day to understand that most of the patients, who were primarily from Afghanistan, had just left, and a new round was due in anytime from Iraq. This was the proverbial "lull in the storm." On my third night there, I teamed up with another reserve chaplain that had been working nonstop for the past nine months. I can't remember his name, but I think he was from South Dakota. His spirits were high, but you could tell that this tour had begun to take its toll on him. I looked deeply into his eyes and wondered if I, too, would look like this after nine months.

He looked thin, with an arresting smile, but hollow eyes. I asked, "So, what do we do?" He said, in an accent I didn't recognize, "Just follow my lead." I waited with him outside the hospital that night — 12:06 a.m., to be exact. I could hear them before I could see them. All of a sudden, he hit me and said, "Let's roll." As I looked up, I saw three sets of brilliant headlights in front of me. They were from big, old blue Air Force school buses that had been turned into ambulances to carry wounded personnel. The buses pulled up right in front of the hospital, and their doors swung open at both ends. Almost in concert, a detail of hospital personnel, dressed in Army Physical Training (PT) gear, began to move stretchers, wheelchairs and crutches into place.

As I drew closer to the buses, my stomach began to knot up. I felt like I was in a lost episode of "M*A*S*H." I could smell them before I could see them. It was very dark under an almost blue-black sky. Out of the corner of my eye, I saw the chaplain pray and board a bus. I was frozen. I could hear someone moaning and someone crying and someone just talking quietly. Walking gently down the aisle of the bus, I could see the chaplain's silhouette. He began to touch everyone he passed and speak in a loving, yet authoritative tone. He announced that they were safe and had arrived in Germany, at an Army hospital — halfway home. The chaplain reassured them that they would be provided the best medical care possible. He continued to tell them that they would soon be able to make a phone call home and eat, and if they wanted prayer, he would visit them as soon as they got settled inside. In closing, he said that it was the *least* we could do for all they had done.

You could see their starry eyes focused in on him. I stood behind him, trying my best to keep my composure. The soldiers were bloody, wounded and half-naked, and some, in great distress. Others were clothed only in their military-issued brown boxers, wrapped up in blue or green old-fashioned wool blankets. Some had their ID cards taped to their forearms. Others had wounds loosely covered with blood-soaked bandages that were falling off. One by one, they were gently off-loaded through the rear of the bus.

Finally, when the bus was emptied, and it was seemingly quiet, I asked, "How often do *you* do this?" His reply was every time a bus comes up the hill or a helicopter lands — sometimes two to three times a day. But, every day, you must be ready. He touched my shoulder and said, "Our job is to provide them with information, encouragement, spiritual guidance and hope." As we started to walk inside to follow up, he turned to me and said, "Whatever you do, give them hope." I knew in that instant what I would be doing for the next year — I would be the honored bearer of hope ... in spite of my fear.

I vowed that I would become that bank of hope immediately. It would not matter to me how I felt or what I saw or how tired I was. It would not matter how much blood there was. It would not matter what uniform they wore, or even if they were civilian. Hope would greet them, eyes opened or eyes closed. Hope would help them inside, and show them how to reach out and touch home. Hope would sit by their bedsides and be a wife, mother, brother or friend until a loved one arrived. Hope would bring them clothes when they were naked. Now, not only was the war real, it was personal.

Thankfulness

"Give thanks with a grateful heart ..."

Growing up in Buffalo, New York, I was taught many life lessons and great pearls of wisdom by my grandmother. One thing she taught me was to say *"Thank you" to everyone who deserved it.* It did not matter to her whether you lived on the rich West Side, or if you slept underneath a park bench. She insisted that if someone did something to help you, your family, or someone else you knew, at the very least, you should open up your mouth and in a pleasant, appreciative tone, and whisper those two magic words. She would say, over and over again, "Don't say it if you don't mean it — nobody likes a liar." We live in a society where so many people are giving lip service to the tradition of "Thank you."

Working daily at a neck-breaking pace, I never had the opportunity to really settle into our small, crowded apartment until late in the summer. Wounded troops poured into the hospital like the steady drip of old molasses. They came, sometimes by the dozens, two or three times a day, with open head injuries that you could smell before you could see. There were young men bent over in pain because they were suffering from kidney stones — a result of the water they had been ingesting — and severely burned patients wrapped in what looked like aluminum foil. Others, looking too old to be at war, came off the buses holding their chests, laboring with every breath. The ones walking had their arms in slings or had skin infections that we could not always cure immediately.

Troops came in every day, and as a unit, we had to formulate a system to off-load everyone in an expeditious fashion. There was no Army manual available to quickly read and train by. We learned, as a team, to rely on "good ole" common sense and the experience of a few rusty, well-worn war vets. We eventually devised a system to help off-load everyone who came for care, and we established a pool of volunteer soldiers who would show up when called on their personal cell phones. (Almost everyone had to purchase a cell phone if they wanted to try and talk to folks here or at home — American cell phones just did not work in Germany.) When called upon, these soldiers would jump out of their bunks, put on their gray-and-black PT gear, and literally run in the pitch dark, using only the light from the American flagpole to lead their way back to the hospital, in order to be ready.

Primarily, the volunteers (and I use the term loosely) were enlisted reserve soldiers who had already worked 12–14 hours in the hospital earlier that day. We were called the "Man Power" detail. The detail needed to have about 20–25 soldiers to work effectively. Some of the Man Power volunteers were assigned to process personnel, others had to push troops in wheelchairs, some had to carry a wounded troop's gear, some had to help assist people walking with crutches, and some (including myself) had to push people on gurneys almost a quarter mile up and down the hallways of this old hospital. Others escorted soldiers to the dining facility for a hot meal, and some just sat with new arrivals as they waited for X-rays or CAT scans. Needless to say, it was a thankless job, day in and day out, sometimes performed two or three times a day.

The entire Chaplain staff was assigned as a permanent fixture to Man Power duty — without choice. We worked together in the cold, rain, sleet, heat and in the snow. There were times when it was so cold that everyone would huddle up just inside the emergency room door and pray for a bus to come before we fell victim to frostbite. On several occasions, because we were so tired from the day's work, we would pray, rap, sing songs, and tell all kinds of jokes in order to stay awake. We did whatever we could so that we wouldn't fall asleep on the job. We needed to contribute our piece for the peace of others.

Even as tired as we were, we stood our post, and we never abandoned our patients. It was during times like these that I remembered what my brother Jerry had taught me early in my college career about learning how to encourage myself. He said to never look for anyone to say "Thank you" for a job well-done, but instead, to learn to pat yourself on your own back, and when necessary, keep on stepping. I tried to convey this philosophy to the Man Power crew, particularly when not enough people showed up to help, or when I saw their motivation waning from the stress and the sadness of all the sickness we saw. Intrinsically, I knew it was my job to keep the distractions to a minimum and keep them focused.

Late one cold night, we were working tirelessly as the rain pounded the roof, hammering out a song we could not recognize. To my surprise — and heart's necessity

— a wounded soldier in a wheelchair, positioned close to the emergency-room door, asked me if he could say a word to the detail. I looked at him, puzzled at the request, and then after conferring with SFC Jones, my senior chaplain assistant, I freely agreed, not really knowing what to expect. What was I thinking? It was extremely wet and cold, not to mention, we were spent already from working. The last thing the Man Power crew needed was to stand in formation in the rain. Nevertheless, something inside of me said to let him speak.

SFC Jones formed everybody up, quickly, in the rain and turned the formation over to the injured soldier. Immediately, he put the formation "at ease" (a relaxed military command for them to listen and not speak). Clutching his side, the injured soldier held his head up high as he began to clear his throat, readying himself to utter anticipated words that would speak through the cold and warm our hearts forever. He opened his mouth and emitted what sounded like a slow Texas drawl. I smiled inwardly as I watched the tears streaming down his face, mixing with the rain that was falling that night.

The wounded sergeant introduced himself and told us that a few nights before; he had arrived at LRMC with a shrapnel injury to his leg, which had caused him excruciating pain. He remembered the kindness and gentleness shown to him, and even though he couldn't walk or talk that night, someone had carried him to his room. He had thought that his duffel bag, with all of his personal belongings and pictures, was lost, but a soldier had found it and brought it to his small, crowded room. He said that someone from the detail pushed him to "chow" (a hot meal), and another soldier helped him take a long, hot shower after days of being left alone in the dirt. The soldier, who looked like General George Patton, said that he was not used to accepting help from anyone. His entire military career over 22 years had been built around being strong and independent. But as he had sat on his bed, late at night, looking out his hospital window, he'd had an epiphany. Even though he was still in pain, he determined that he would roll himself downstairs from the farthest ward in the hospital, in the rain, to say "Thank you" to us for a job well-done in difficult times.

There are no existing words that can describe the faces in the formation after his speech. These were deployed soldiers, primarily reservists, who were severely overworked, underpaid, all alone and extremely tired. They felt unappreciated and misused, and had begun to wonder aloud, to themselves and others, what they had gotten themselves into by being in Germany in the middle of a real war. A great force from a sincere heart energized these soldiers. Someone had actually taken the time to acknowledge and notice their hard work and sacrifice, and it was priceless. Some were teary-eyed at this unsolicited gratitude; some had smiles a mile wide. You could sense immediately that a new day was dawning in their hearts. What a golden moment — an eclipse where the light of gratitude had penetrated the darkness. I knew then that we would make it through at least this part of the deployment — all because someone uttered those two powerful words: "Thank you."

The Apartment

"A house is not always a home ..."

Eight hundred twelve Union Street was the address of the crooked, old white house on a small hill that I lived in while attending Valparaiso University. It was a two-bedroom, two-story rental house off of the main drag. The house had a half porch and a small, dark, musty basement. It also had a tiny storage room off the kitchen that was supposed to be a pantry, but we creatively turned it into a luxury suite for one lucky co-ed. Of course, for us, luxury had nothing to do with amenities and everything to do with solitude. It was the only single bedroom in the house. We had enough furniture to make the place look lived-in and comfy. We didn't lack for beds or tables or chairs. And we really didn't care if any of the furniture matched, as long as it performed its primary function.

For almost two years, I lived in and shared this home with three wonderful African-American women, who became my closest friends and sorority sisters (go pink and green!!). Anita was from Gary, Indiana. She had a ton of brothers and sisters, and her mom owned a small beauty shop and from time to time would give us the college discount on our hairdos. I learned from Anita what maturity looked like at a young age and not to be afraid to try. Anita was wise about the truths of life at an early age; she was the only one with what I would call a "real" job, as a salesperson for a beauty-product company. Briana was the life of the party and the youngest of all of us. She came to "Valpo" for a degree and was determined not to go home without it. I always remember her typing fast and writing long papers so many nights. She was an English major and had big dreams of becoming a lawyer. She taught me that "big was beautiful" long before Monique and that too many people in life were more concerned with the wrapping instead of the gift inside. Dorothy Jean, my best friend out of the trio, was from Columbia, Maryland. Her mom was a college professor and a single parent. Dorothy taught to me to never quit. She encouraged me to stay in school when I wanted to leave for a better-paying job at IBM. She propped me up when I would get down on myself. When I didn't have any money, she loaned me money that she had gotten from her grandmother for something else. And, when I didn't have a place to go after graduation, because I was too embarrassed to go home unemployed, she volunteered her old bedroom in her mom's house. There, I would have the chance at a fresh start. Dorothy was selfless, an exquisite listener, with a heart as big as heaven. At a pivotal point in my life, I remember her telling me how she saw glimpses of my success, and that all I had to do was believe and hang in there.

We all came from different stock, but together we were a fabulous team. We were your consummate starving college students, but we thought we could do anything. Sometimes, at the end of the month, we were so poor that we would draw straws to see who would write the "bounced" check for food at the local grocery store. It didn't matter that we all worked and went to school, because we never seemed to have enough to make it. We shared our living expenses, and at the end of every month, Dorothy or Briana would divide up the utility bills and tell us how much we each owed. The phone bill was always the killer; a house full of women on a phone constantly can be a scary proposition.

Living at 812 was just plain old fun. Over the years, we had a few small house parties with food, friends and funk music, where we loved to imitate Diana Ross and the Supremes and sing "Ain't No Mountain High Enough." Also for fun, we would climb into Dorothy's 1965 maroon, four-door Chevy with the ignition on the panel and drive to Chicago (40 miles away) to sneak into a dance club for some special celebration. When we did have some money, we tried to plan a big barbecue complete with chicken, potato salad, watermelon and anything else we could find. At 812, I learned how to share, how to listen, and how to love other women who were different from me. It was an experience that I carried in my heart everywhere I went in my adult life. It was something I loved to talk and laugh about with young college students that were coming along. Though it was a memorable time in my life, it was not an experience that I ever wanted to live physically through again, particularly at age 43.

Never say never! I assumed that since Landstuhl was a long-established Army community and hospital with a hotel, that we would be put up in officer's quarters. I half-jokingly expected to "bunk up" with one other female officer in a one-bedroom, one-bath apartment — after all; those were the arrangements when I first started out in 1984 as a second lieutenant. I just knew that my living situation would be fair, if not good. As it turned out, I was assigned to live in an old, vacant, brick; four-story, enlisted family-housing building that had been emptied and slated for interior destruction.

When we first got off the buses at Landstuhl, we were ushered into a small waiting area in the training building to receive our quarters. A sergeant screamed, "Just listen for your name, come and get your keys, and go to your 'new home.'" As I sat waiting, my palms began to get very sweaty; I noticed that all of the other female field-grade officers (major through colonel) had been assigned rooms and left, whereas I was still waiting. I asked one of the supply soldiers, "What about me?" She smiled and said, "Ma'am, don't worry. We have a space for you, but we were a bit confused." She said that they were told to house all of the chaplains together because of the nature of our work (counseling, late-night hours, confidentiality, etc.) The unit had given the two male chaplains a room to themselves and had assigned me to live with them, until some high-speed soldier figured out I was a female chaplain.

No one at the unit had seen a female chaplain before and assumed that the title on the roster was wrong.

They all thought it was a typo and that I was Captain Hopkins *not* Chaplain (Major) Hopkins. So after all of the assignments had been made, they found out that I was in fact a female chaplain. They had to scurry around to find a bed for me. I was assigned a leftover space with a group of seven captain nurses. The unit didn't know what else to do with me, and they were praying that the *nurses* would be okay with having me as a roommate. I laughed!

I smiled and asked for the keys. As the senior ranking person in the apartment, it would be my responsibility to sign for all of the Army property. Normally, when you go overseas as a soldier, you can only take so much furniture. Therefore, the Army supplies most major items and when you leave, they come and count their stuff to make sure you didn't sell it or give it away.

So I took the key and followed the trail of people about a half mile from the hospital over to our new home. I signed for all of the common-use furniture in the apartment — a table, six chairs, eight bunk beds, a rug, two couches, a refrigerator and a stove.

There wasn't anything else in the apartment. I went to the room alone and looked around, thinking, "Is this it? Whose bright idea was this? How are we going to live like this with barely enough stuff to make it a home?" After traveling 12 days and 14 hours, I stood motionless in a seemingly barren apartment and prayed that things would quickly get better than this. I was saddened and shocked, but I knew I couldn't let anyone see my real feelings.

I ran back down the hill, through the mud, and gathered my roommates to lead them to our "new" place. It was a washed-beige, barely supplied, almost-condemned, mildew-smelling place. The upside was that it was on the third floor and at the end of the building, so hopefully, we wouldn't have to contend with a lot of apartment noise. I was trying desperately to find a silver lining. I knew that all of my roommates were trained professional women, from established homes and communities, who had been living middle- to upper-middle-class lives. In the blink of an eye, they had been snatched out of their comfort zones and thrown into this seemingly dismal living situation. As they each walked into the apartment, one by one, I could see the look of disappointment in their eyes. Each one was so tired that she couldn't even complain. All they could do was find a bunk and go to sleep.

When it came to living in this space, we had to quickly figure out how to make lemonade out of lemons. The first thing was to make a list of things we needed to survive and establish some basic rules. We were very fortunate to have women who wanted to work together. Some apartments fought from day one about the most mundane of things. They fought about phone service, TV times, room-visitation policies, food storage, cooking and even men.

As a group, we were committed to peace. We didn't necessarily know or like each other yet, but we would have peace in our place. Initially, we made up teams and went out during the next couple of days to acquire what we needed to upgrade our apartment. We purchased items from thrift stores; we got donations from regular Army folks who took pity on us or got stuff right off the German streets. Luckily, and quickly, we found a television, a DVD player, a microwave, a toaster, pots, pans, dishes, rugs and a shower curtain. We had each brought our own blankets and extra sheets; mine were from my kids' room, so I slept on Winnie the Pooh and SpongeBob for a year. It was time for us, as women, to get creative, not to lie down, mope or cry.

We were given meal cards in order to eat daily in the hospital, but the kitchen was closed after 7 p.m. If you were working late, were busy, or a bus came in, you couldn't leave patients just to go eat; we missed a lot of meals (breakfast, lunch and dinner). When we didn't work, we had to walk over to the hospital in the cold, rain and snow, just to eat. So we decided to try and build a kitchen that was useful. We had to buy everything. We bought salt, pepper, sugar, coffee, tea, flour, rice, cinnamon, detergent, Clorox, buckets, mops, etc. Once, we bought so much stuff that we had to put the bags on the mop handle just to carry them about a mile back to the room. Everyone had their own assigned cabinet to put their personal food items in, like candy, Pop-Tarts, soda and snacks. We didn't have much space, but it was enough.

To keep the arguing down and the cleanliness up, we also decided to make a weekly cleanup roster for the common-use areas. (This changed over the course of the year, but the system proved to be indispensable.) The ladies quickly realized that when you live in a small space with a lot of other women with different schedules, you must learn to be accommodating of each other. One of our biggest "bones" of contention was when to run that "doggone" dryer.

How do you keep eight women happy for a year in close quarters? Well, you learn to keep the television on low for Joan. Cheryl and Marisol would listen to their favorite movies and soaps with their noses six inches away from the TV screen. We also didn't talk much on our cell phones in common areas. We would go outside on the balcony, in the middle of winter, to talk. We bought a German house-phone plan because it was cheaper than what the military and AT&T could offer us to call home. Vonetta insisted that we not slam the kitchen-cabinet doors in the mornings (she worked nights). I wanted clean bathrooms and a clean kitchen, so I spent extra time cleaning them without complaining. Nadine and Aretha needed the place cool whenever possible — they lived in the hot-flash zone, with the windows open and the fan on in the middle of the winter. Little things became deal breakers. My cell would ring off the hook some nights, and I was constantly going and coming at all hours, so I ended up in the smallest room by myself — both a blessing and a curse — but it all worked out.

By the time a couple of months went by, we were cozy and comfy. We had transformed that sad apartment into a place where we could rest from a long day of work. We had flowers on the table; we had matching shower curtains and rugs and all the girly smell-good stuff to go with it — not to mention, the best cooks in the village. Our neighbors were jealous and could be found knocking on our door at the smell of Aretha's homemade rolls, Vonetta's lasagna and seven-flavor pound cake, or Nadine's secret Arkansas potato salad. It was not something we wanted to do, but we were able to do it well — kind of like 812.

Love

"... And the greatest of these is love."

True love is very hard to find. It is not lust. It is not the kind of love that has a high physical attraction, but a short life span. I believe that everyone ought to experience true love at least once. At some point in your lifetime, your heart ought to stop and skip a few beats at the mention of someone else's name, and everyone's eyes ought to be wide with desire when someone you are madly in love with graces your door. True love is not seasonal or convenient, it is not harsh or bitter, and it is good even in bad times. It is a whisper that calms your soul in the middle of a crushing storm. True love props you up when you fall down, and it has the power to forgive, restore; mend broken hearts and to heal.

He was a helicopter pilot, a warrant officer, who's helicopter got caught up in some wires and landed near a riverbed deep enough to drown in. We were told by some witnesses from the scene that the pilot had been underwater for what seemed like a long time, maybe 10 minutes or more. When he arrived by medevac at LRMC, the young warrant officer was unconscious and in very critical condition. His name was Mac and he had not been blown up or shot at. He didn't have a sucking chest wound or even a severe bloody head wound. Lying on his gurney, Mac looked like he was taking a peaceful nap, almost too peaceful. The young pilot had been under the water for too long, and the initial prevailing thought was that he had suffered some severe brain damage and had reached a point of no return. We all were deeply concerned. I undoubtedly knew that something was terribly wrong with him, but somehow I felt at peace, almost like the tranquility you feel when you sit by a lake on a calm, quiet day. This feeling was inexplicable, because here he was, a soldier injured in the war, now very seriously ill. Even though he didn't look ill, he was. As we changed his bloody dressings and cleaned his wounds, I had an overwhelming feeling that everything would be all right. Even though I couldn't say it out loud then to anyone, I really felt it in my heart.

After Mac was settled in, we quickly went about the arduous task of locating his family members to notify them of his whereabouts and his present condition.

We quickly located his wife, Sharon, and she agreed to come as soon as possible. She arrived exhausted and anxious to see her love. She knew her husband had been hurt badly in a helicopter accident and had been rushed to Germany for treatment, but she did not know the details of his injuries. Right away, you could tell that she knew the importance of listening and asking good questions as the doctor briefed her. Sharon had only brought a small backpack on her journey, even though it was the dead of winter. We showed her to Mac's room and she stood by his bedside, where he was critical, yet still peaceful looking. The doctors initially explained that he had experienced severe head trauma on impact, and had the effects of someone who had been drowned. She was informed that Mac was also in a deep coma. Sharon shook as she heard the news, and then asked for a chair to sit next to his bedside. After watching her for a while, I left her to be alone with him.

I returned later to peek in on her and offer any support that I could — a hug, a listening ear, a prayer, whatever she wanted. I knew the gravity of the situation and desperately wanted her not to feel alone. I had noticed how hard it was for several family members of patients in the ICU not to have anyone close to them around. I also noticed that Sharon didn't have a sweater or jacket on and it was cool in the ICU, so I brought her a sweat top to stay warm. She was very appreciative of everything that was being done, but the longer she stayed, the more being in the ICU took its toll on her. After awhile, she looked worn, tired and pale. Day after day, Mac didn't move, he didn't respond to the sound of her voice, or to the touch of her hand. She stayed in the fight and stayed focused, refusing to give in or give up. The determination was in her steel-blue eyes, if you really paid attention. She made a sanctuary out of his room, for the both of them. She brought beautiful pictures of their children playing baseball, with friends and family members. There were notes written in an elementary hand, and pictures of rainbows and butterflies, colored with bright markers and paints.

Sharon would sit endlessly for hours, reading to him whatever she could find, whether it was news, sports or the weather. She would also have long one-sided conversations about their love, their life and most importantly, their future. I saw her gently bathe him when the nurses were too busy. She would massage his feet every night and pray (*I would imagine*) that this too would pass. Sharon didn't have much, but all that she had, she put into healing him.

Sadly, it looked like all of her efforts would not be enough. When I visited the room, I could see the tension in her neck and hear the fear in her voice. Here was a woman torn and desperately afraid. The man she loved looked like he was on the brink of no return. I could sense that this wasn't just another ordinary married couple; they were a pair very much in love with each other. Although she never uttered these words to me, her actions said it all. I could tell that Mac was *IT* for her and that she was not ready for him to go.

After a few long nights, I found Sharon in a chair by Mac's bedside sobbing. There had been no noticeable improvement and things were looking bleak. It was like a scene from a movie where you know the plot is about to thicken and climax to an unforgettable ending. Lord knows, I didn't want to be in on a sad ending now, but I had just been asked by her doctors to go get her so they could talk with her in the comfort room. The comfort room — what an oxymoron — it was the place we took people to tell them bad news about their loved ones.

Sharon looked at me as I spoke. She got up and nodded, but she hesitated long enough to kiss Mac's cheek and whisper in his ear for him not to go anywhere because she would be right back. The doctors and staff wanted her to be made aware of her death benefits; and they wanted her permission to begin the paperwork to retire Mac as soon as possible so that when, not if, he passed, she would receive a retirement pension instead of just his death benefits. It really was an act of compassion on their part, but she wasn't quite ready to throw the towel in. Sharon asked if she could have some more time to think, and of course, they said yes.

I have rarely seen such commitment, such care, such tenderness, such patience and such devotion all in one. As a person of faith, I like to always keep hope alive, but even I was growing afraid for them. I can't remember exactly how long after the comfort-room visit it happened, but something wonderful occurred. Mac woke up. When he opened his eyes, he was weary, sore, and unsure of what he had been through, but even in his haze, he looked up and recognized his love. Tears of joy streamed down Sharon's pale skin. She gently reached for him and touched his forehead, trying not to disturb any of the apparatus around him. Her husband had turned the corner on death. A modern-day triumph over adversity — the pilot was yet alive. It was indeed a miracle, and I will always believe that somewhere deep inside, this soldier heard his love calling for him and fought his way back. He fought all the way from death's door back to the heart of his queen. Brave Heart didn't have anything on this couple.

As I watched this drama unfold, I began to reflect. I leafed through the recesses of my heart to draw out the story of love that taught me about never quitting until you have what you want. I closed my eyes and smiled as I remembered chasing my high school sweetheart, Jay, halfway around the world and into the Army. He was a tall, dark, dreamy, cup-of-latte, West Point–graduate Infantry Ranger who was on his way to Germany to serve a three-year tour; and I wanted so much to be with him that I quit my job as the first black female recruit at the Police Academy in Howard County, Maryland. I quit after having been in training for only about four weeks. The community was so excited that I had finally crossed the racial barrier that they wrote an article about me in the local newspaper, but I would not be swayed. I packed up all my things, left Maryland, and joined the Army as Private First Class Pringle.

I was an enlisted soldier, even though I had a college degree. I told my mom and family that I joined so that I could pay off my college loans and have an opportunity to see the world. They thought I was crazy to give up the police academy. Secretly, I thought I was crazy, too. But I had different dreams, dreams of being loved, dreams of getting married, and dreams of getting transferred to Germany so I could see Jay every day and lay my head upon his chest. We had been an item throughout college, and strangely enough, we always had a relationship where we had to deal with distance. It seemed like a daunting task at 23, but I thought, "I am young and in love, and if not now, then when?" This dream burned a hole in my soul, and I pursued it with relentless abound. I put everything else in my life on hold. Nothing and no one mattered more than he. I didn't really understand what it would take to become an officer. I just figured that if I worked hard enough, it would come my way. I went to basic training at Fort Dix, New Jersey. After graduating, I was put on a bus and sent to Fort Devens, Massachusetts, to learn Morse code at my Advanced Initial Training (AIT). This was almost a failure — copying Morse code was something you had to do by instinct, not by thought, and I was the classic thinker. It was a grueling 20-plus week course, and daily, I felt my dream slipping away as I would fail a test and then retake it to stay afloat. But through determination, tenacity and the grace of God, I prevailed and got offered an opportunity to go immediately to Officer Candidate School (OCS) in Georgia.

My prayers had been answered, and if all went well, I would be an officer and on my way to Germany, into the arms of my beloved, in less than 16 more weeks. At OCS, I worked like a mad woman. I only slept about four hours a night; I studied tactics and map-reading in the bathroom at night by the lights that never went off. I learned to run two miles in 13 minutes or less. And every day, I was motivated by my dream and inspired by the picture of Jay I had tucked in the top of my hat, which I took everywhere — to classes in the Infantry building, to the rifle range, the obstacle course, the repelling tower, to kitchen duty at 4 a.m. and on those long 20-mile road marches. I would remind myself daily that nothing would stop me from reaching my goal. After 16 weeks, I graduated — as the top female Leadership graduate (not bad for a girl chasing a dream of love) — and got my choice of assignments. You guessed it ... I went to Germany! Love had found a way. It wouldn't be long before the two of us were married and living out my dream.

It took me close to 18 months to get to my love. Sharon had to endure eight long, unpredictable days in an ICU. Love is something that is amazing, powerful, motivational and long-suffering. As I watched Sharon and Mac board their bus to leave, I thought secretly that if their love was the kind of love we saw day in and day out, then as a world and as a people, we would be so much better — and maybe, just maybe, not at war.

Honor

"All is lost except for honor"

Even though people die in every war, I don't think anyone actually goes to war thinking it will be them. Unfortunately, after the first round is fired and the line of demarcation is crossed, we all know that someone will surely get hurt or die. Someone will give their life so that you and I don't have to.

As I ate my oatmeal or cooked-to-order omelet every morning in the mess hall, I would try and find a seat in front of the big-screen television in the back corner to get my daily report on the action in Iraq. I actually depended on the folks at CNN Europe and FOX News for a lot of my war updates. I was mostly interested in who or what was blown up so I could ascertain how many injured troops we might be getting in the middle of the next night. I watched the news like most who had been "temporarily" deployed — hoping to hear about anything that would mean we could pack up and go home soon: a cease-fire, a peace treaty or a surrender agreement. As I watched daily, I took mental notes of those who had been killed in action. It may sound strange, but I knew that if someone from the 1st Armored Division was killed, I might be called to do their funeral/memorial service here before they went home to the States.

The 1st Armored Division was stationed in Baumholder, Germany, which was about 30 miles from LRMC, and when they were mobilized to go to Iraq, the chaplains were informed that we might have to receive any fallen soldiers from that unit. Receiving fallen soldiers wasn't something I did all the time; most fallen soldiers would fly directly to Andrews Air Force Base in Maryland. But, because Germany was their assigned home, it would be necessary from time to time to receive soldiers from this unit. Germany was the place where the soldier had left and the place where loved ones awaited their safe return.

As I recall, it was a beautiful, sunny day the first time we were asked to receive a fallen hero. We were given a warning order (advance notice) that a soldier from the 1st Armored Division had died and would be coming in immediately. Most of the chaplains from this unit were deployed, and the few reservists assigned back here were so busy they wouldn't be able to get to the soldier in time, so in true fashion, we were asked to help out.

Once I was officially told to go, I had the detail go with me, and believe it or not, there was no problem getting 15 soldiers who wanted to go and help. Even if they had just finished a 12- or 14-hour shift, most of them considered it an honor to be asked. I sent my chaplain assistant out to gather up transportation for us and to let everyone know where we would meet. We all changed into fresh, starched uniforms and shiny boots, and hopped into our vehicles for the quick ride over to the air base. We had to wear our best everyday Battle Dress (green camouflage) Uniform, or BDU, because we did not come to Germany with our Class A (green dress) uniforms. We were only allowed to bring two duffel bags and a carry-on with all of the gear needed to fight. I guess it didn't occur to our planner that we would ever have to dress up for any occasion as soldiers. It could've been possible that no one really thought we would be in this war long enough for so many to lose their lives.

The detail drove to the flight line in almost complete silence, and upon arrival, we were escorted to a clean, sterile-looking waiting room. We were told to wait there to receive the fallen hero once the aircraft arrived. As we waited, my heart began beating like a drum that was echoing deep in the woods. Quietly, I rehearsed my lines (the Army has protocol for every occasion), silently said my prayers, and chose the scriptures I would read. Standing alone in the corner of the room, I realized that even though I had for years been preaching the gospel weekly to hundreds back home, this service could potentially be one of my most sacred moments. For me, it was a time to reflect on the service and sacrifice of this young man, and to render unto him every bit of honor and respect owed him for his duty.

After the plane touched down and taxied to the designated location, we were all summoned to get up and get moving. Diligently, we climbed into a miniature blue shuttle bus as the vehicle following closely behind us carried the remains of the fallen hero. As we rode out to meet the plane, it seemed that everything and everyone slowed down and stopped. People that were working on the flight turned toward us and glanced with their heads and eyes turned down in reverence. It was as if they knew we were going to retrieve one of our own, and as we rode, you could hear the wind whisper and the tires thump against the dry, gray road.

The airplane was a large civilian plane like a 737, except it was almost completely stripped down on the inside — it had no seats, no overhead compartments and no carpet. It looked like it had been hollowed out just to accommodate the oversized silver box that the hero lay in. I cannot explain the feeling you have when you approach a large, metal box that is draped in a flag that you know, and honor, with the body of someone just like you in it. For a moment, you think to yourself, "But for the grace of God, there go I," and you realize that this is not some made-up event, but instead a comrade who paid the ultimate sacrifice. I could see the soldiers quickly wipe away the tears as they fell, and feel the swelling in our hearts as we stood still and silent in his presence. Once we identified the fallen hero, we humbly encircled his gray, steel box and prepared to proceed. The soldiers reached down and grabbed the stiffening, ice-cold metal case as if it were room temperature. I moved to the position of honor, the head, and said a short prayer. After the prayer, the detail quickly stood to attention and followed the instructions of the Air Force technician as if they were delicately holding a brand-new baby.

The entire time I was on the plane, I was mesmerized by the solemnity of it all. I caught myself drifting back to May 1976, and the day of my grandmother's funeral. My grandmother had helped to raise me after my parents divorced, when I was five, and she had been, for all intents and purposes, my best friend. She was quiet, strong, gorgeous and handy. She was a great cook, a pillar of our church, a gardener, and a friend to all who met her. Then all of a sudden in March of 1976, while I was gone at school, she fell unconscious in our home and experienced several strokes that would leave her paralyzed and unable to verbally communicate with us the last two months of her life. I remember going to the Erie County Medical Center, day in and day out, watching her lie lifelessly on her cold, gray, metal bed in a ward with eight other very sick women. I would talk to her and play music for her, wanting her to come alive again and just sit up and tell me everything would be all right. I wanted her to be healed and well again. But, it was not going to happen. The doctors told my mother that her prognosis was not good and that she had only a few weeks to live. I wanted to be near my grandmother every day, so I volunteered to become a Red Cross Candy Striper. But on day number 59, she died of complications from her strokes while still in the hospital. When I was allowed to see her, all I could do was cry and think that my hero was now gone. All I could think about was "why her," when there were so many other people who I honestly felt could leave this world and no one would really care.

The plane, the casket, the soldier brought it all flooding back to me. I was standing in the plane, going through the motions, yet questioning the value of this soldier's death, this war, while thinking about the pain of my own 27-year-old wound. I wondered if those that loved him would feel like I felt when my grandmother died — cheated. I shook my head and began to read from my Bible, "Yea, though I walk through the valley of the shadow of death, I will fear no evil, for thou art with me," until it occurred to me that the words were not coming out. I started again aloud and prayed for strength to continue. It took about 12 soldiers to move the fallen hero in this oversized steel container safely off the plane into a transport vehicle and out to his unit. Every time this fallen hero was moved, we saluted and rendered him honor, and not once did we leave his side until he made it safely back to the morgue. It was a hard task for me, but on that plane, a new day dawned and healing began to take route.

It is difficult to eulogize someone you don't know when someone you do know is floating through your head, heart and soul. When my mind began to wander, I worried that I might fail this fallen hero, that I would be preoccupied and not give him enough honor, respect, attention or time.

But as I continued, I felt a calm come over me and a sense of relief. I knew everything would be OK. I slowly raised my head and proceeded to the front of the casket, and with peace and great honor, I continued this short ceremony. Honor is an earned right; no one goes to war to die, but when it happens, we must always remember each fallen hero with dignity and respect. And, for those of us who have our own wounds to heal, we must put them aside and do the job that has been placed in front of us. Maybe in doing the work, we will find healing and peace. I know I did.

Everybody Counts

"I am Somebody ..."

When I was five years old, my parents separated. We were living in San Francisco, California, and my mother decided to pack up my two brothers, Frank and Jerry, and myself and take us to New York to live. I don't remember much about the trip except that we went on a long Amtrak train ride for days through various places. The black porters were nice to us, teaching us card games and giving us extra Shirley Temple drinks throughout the day. I distinctly remember going through Chicago, Illinois, where I saw a group of sailors and where my brother Jerry and I would get money by digging in phones booths for the leftover change. After the long ride, we all settled in Buffalo, New York, with my maternal grandmother. Granny lived in and ran a lime-green rooming house for single men with a metal rod fence all around it. The men's rooms were upstairs, and we all lived in a three-bedroom flat downstairs. Over the years, we helped Granny clean the house, can apple butter and tomatoes, cook scrumptious soul-food meals on a budget, and wash clothes on her hand-wringing machine in the basement. She also taught us how to raise vegetables, grapes and rhubarb in a backyard city garden. The neighborhood we lived in was poor, but clean. There were bums who played checkers on the corner. We had the traditional local corner store, "Mr. O'Hare," where you could buy things on credit until your monthly check came in. It was nothing to find alcohol or gambling going on just about anywhere near our house. We played in the streets and rode the bus, or family friends with cars would pick us up and take us to church or other places. My mother worked hard for her money. She got up every day and caught the Broadway Street bus to Elmwood and the Elmwood Street bus to work. She worked literally all the way across town at the University bookstore, where she barely made enough to pay all the bills. I could imagine that as time rolled on, she looked at her surroundings and dreamt about something better for her children.

My brothers had been going to a local Boys Club miles away from home to box and play baseball. It was there that they had some positive black male role models, but that wasn't enough for my mother; there wasn't enough mentoring or security for her.

So my mom called my dad, who lived 150 miles away in Ohio, and they decided that it would be best if my brothers would go and live with him. Daddy was a milkman who worked for the Sealtest Milk Company. He owned a beige, two-story home in East Cleveland, Ohio — the suburbs. All three of us would go and visit him in the summer nearly every year. Compared to where we lived, daddy's place was wonderful. During the summers we spent in East Cleveland, Daddy would sign us up for swimming lessons at the public pool and take us out afterward to Burger King ... where it took "two hands to handle the Whopper." He even had a green Lincoln Continental with suicide doors, and we were excited anytime daddy took us for a ride in it.

As I take myself back, I sit here now and remember the day like it was yesterday. I was in the dining room, behind my grandmother's long buffet cabinet near the bathroom door, when I saw my parents on the couch long in conversation. It looked like an intense, but cordial conversation. I kept asking myself "what are they talking about?" The conversation ended just as quickly as it had begun. The side door to the house was open and my brothers had their suitcases in their hands. I knew now that my dad had come for them. Frank and Jerry were going to live permanently with my dad –no one had to tell me anything. I was staying in Buffalo to live with my mom and my grandmother. My heart stopped for what felt like an eternity. I loved my brothers with every fiber of my being, and I had never been separated from them both at the same time. I was still sharing a room with Jerry, who was only 11 months my senior. I was so young; my world as I knew it came to a crushing halt. For days, weeks, months, and yes, even years, after that incident, I felt like an outsider, I was all alone. My mom and grandmother would still be there, but I was the child left behind, the one left standing by the buffet cabinet without a suitcase. I fought back the tears as they closed the door and walked slowly down the sidewalk, away.

Have you ever been left behind? If you have, then you will know exactly how theses troops lying inside a hot transport bus felt. The second group of POWs from the 507th Maintenance Company had been given a special bus to take them and their escorts over to the flight line. The POWs, by and large, were ambulatory and needed little assistance, which was great news. As they were getting on their bus and I was saying goodbye to them, I noticed out of the corner of my eye another blue transport bus waiting along the gray brick wall, about 15 feet away, with wounded troops on stretchers. I thought to myself, "This can't be an incoming bus — what is it doing over there?" My curiosity had been peaked, so I said goodbye and quickly excused myself from the POWs. I ran over to see what was going on. As I hopped on the bus, I saw a mixture of wounded soldiers. There were at least three badly wounded young men and a couple sitting right up front with some superficial wounds. They looked like a group of happy campers who were ready to break camp and go home. As I said hello, I could hear a mixture of clapping and sneering from way in the back of the bus. Two soldiers turned to each other and in unison said, "Oh no, you lost, pay up." "What?" I asked. Another soldier, laughing, said, "He isn't talking to you ma'am" and began to tell me exactly what was going on. He said, "We noticed that everybody — doctors, nurses, staff, and a bunch of high-ranking Army officials came out to say goodbye to the POWs and congratulate them once more. We also noticed that the hospital even gave them their own bus to ride on back to the flight line, but not us; they just left us over here in the sun waiting, crowded, until they were ready to go.

"So we started thinking out loud, isn't losing a leg or getting shot in the butt, or getting shrapnel through your eye enough for someone, anyone, to come and shake our hands and say goodbye?" he said. "So, we made a friendly wager that no one from that 'goodbye detail' would come and say anything to us, but my friend here remembered you from when he came in late last week. He said, 'That little ole "crazy" black chaplain took the time to speak to everyone when I got here, and I bet she will come and say something to us before we leave.' The bet was $20 apiece, and we all just lost when you hopped on the bus."

To say that there was a lump in my throat would be an understatement. I tried to make a joke about whether I would get all the money, but it was time for them to go. So I walked down the aisle and shook everyone's hands, and with tears in my eyes, said, "Thanks for your sacrifice, good luck, goodbye, and may God richly bless you." I made it look like I had planned it all along, but the truth was, I was one minute from failing them. One minute from forgetting to honor their service and their loss. The tears were because I was ashamed; the tears were from an 11-year-old girl still standing alone by the buffet cabinet.

I remembered as I wept that everybody counts and that sometimes, we only choose to remember those who are like us, or those who make us feel better or look better, or those who make the news. Yes, it was true that the POWs made national headlines, but before I left LRMC, I would see over 12,000 injured troops and close to 350 in the ICU. I would look daily into the eyes of hundreds who honestly just wanted to know that they mattered and that their service counted. We don't have the right to discount anyone, and the one thing I know for sure is that when you do discount someone, you leave a wound that no medicine can cure. Our troops are being wounded physically every day, in ways that will leave visible scars to all who care to look. Let us promise, as a nation, not to leave scars that go undetected deep inside, simply because we forgot that their service matters, and that everybody who serves counts.

Perseverance

"Don't Quit ..."

Every time I opened the doors to the ICU, I knew that someone needed help. It might have been a nurse or doctor who had lost too many patients that week, or it might have been a mother or father sitting quietly by the bedside of a child they loved dearly who was now nonresponsive. It might have been a soldier crying uncontrollably, looking to purge the atrocities they had seen, or done, in Iraq. This is a story about someone I needed to meet — a real hero, a soldier who wanted people to know that he would not quit.

I didn't know his name or even his rank; all I knew was what I heard. He was in the first room on the right by the backdoor of the ICU. He had been heavily sedated at first, but after a few days, he had begun to come around. He talked a little to some of the nurses and doctors in the unit, just trying to get his bearings. This nameless soldier has a story of perseverance and encouragement.

While out on a patrol with his unit, outside of a small Iraqi town, a deadly RPG (rocket-propelled grenade) exploded inside his Humvee. His driver was killed immediately, but miraculously, he survived. Shrapnel had exploded into his face, arms and neck. Blood was flowing everywhere. He couldn't feel his hands or his feet, but he could see them and knew they were still attached. There was blood smeared all over the windows inside the cab of the vehicle. The soldier said he had felt like he was floating away, like in those dreams about dying. He didn't want to go. As quickly as he closed his eyes, he caught a glimpse of his beautiful little girl, thousands of miles away, calling his name; and instantaneously, he willed himself to live. He would not give up. He didn't mind leaving his unit, but he couldn't bear the fact of leaving his daughter, who was probably sound asleep at home, without a father. So, silently, the soldier prayed for help.

Quickly, he gathered himself and made a plan. After what seemed like an eternity, he tried to get himself out of the damaged vehicle. The flimsy-material door was jammed, so he pushed it once, hard, with his backside, and it flung wide open. The soldier could hear some small-arms fire in the distance, and he thought for sure that someone from his unit would still be around fighting. In his mind, he recalled what had been taught in basic training: "never leave your ranger buddy behind."

The soldier managed to get out of the vehicle and drag himself onto the ground. Immediately after hitting the ground, he heard muffled sounds, like the voices of Iraqi soldiers, rapidly approaching. Using his natural survival instinct, he determined to play dead until they passed. But they were closer than he thought, and one of them took a potshot at his head — just for the hell of it, he supposed. The soldier heard the shot but felt no pain, and after being on the ground for a while, he slowly opened his eyes, realizing that they had hit his Kevlar helmet.

The shots had missed his head — he was given yet another chance. So, once again, he got up, against all odds, and dragged himself through the dirt and sand. Finally, after an unknown amount of time, he awoke in a tent that smelled like a hospital. He was fading in and out of consciousness on a stretcher surrounded by people speaking English. He wasn't sure where he was, but it felt like friendly territory. Eventually, he was to find out that he was indeed in an Army field hospital called a CASH (Combat Army Support Hospital). From there, he was expeditiously airlifted to LRMC. The soldier had survived; he was alive and determined to share his remarkable story.

Every day, I would go *by*, but not *in*, this soldier's room. I was feeling down most of the time, but his presence and his story (that I had heard second hand) helped me keep my situation in perspective.

An RPG (Rocket Propelled Grenade) hadn't blown me up, an unknown enemy hadn't shot a live round at me, and I wasn't bleeding profusely from some orifice. Neither was I strapped to a gurney, grasping for my last breath, inside a cold, noisy aircraft speeding toward safety. I was alive and unwounded. Deployed? Yes. Lonely? Yes. I was exhausted and tired already of seeing strong young men and women blown apart. It was barely April — one month into the war. I had painted a happy face on the outside and fooled most everyone I knew. But the truth was that my inner being ached and longed for the comforts of home. Deep within, I felt like I was changing, becoming a different person. It almost felt as if day by day, trial by trial, I was slowly dying, but the story of this soldier woke me up. It taught me that everyone has a job to do in war; like it or not, this was mine. It was, in a strange way, an epiphany — I realized that I needed to stop feeling sorry for myself.

I was grown and had volunteered years ago to serve, even if I had not volunteered for this war. I determined deep within that as long as I had breath in my lungs and blood running through my veins, I would make this experience count. I would pull myself back together mentally and go to work. I pledged that I would work as hard as I could at LRMC. I was convinced that there would not be a task beneath me or above me; as a chaplain, I would empty bedpans to help nurses, I would hold poles in the operating rooms to help wash out wounds, and I would feed soldiers from their bedside trays. I would help serve meals when others were not available. I would push wheelchairs stuck in the hallway. And when the need arose, I would hold a soldier and cry with them until the pain passed. It was the least I could do for all that had been done during this time. I was determined to not only overcome, but to also persevere.

Perseverance is something I learned a long time ago. It is what took a ghetto girl from Buffalo, New York, through four years of college in Indiana. I remember the end of my freshman year when I received my grades. Admittedly, I had partied more than I had studied, but I was smart and had assumed that I would make it anyhow. So imagine my surprise when I opened the envelope for my grades to find out that my GPA was a 1.9 (out of 4). I was shocked and horrified — this meant I would have to pack up and go home. Suddenly, my life flashed before me, reminding me of all the odds that were against me. No one at home had any money, and now, here I was about to be on a path that I did not want to be on. I didn't know what to do, but I refused to give in, because I didn't want to work at Bethlehem Steel, or the Chevy Plant. I wanted my life to be different. I wanted my life to be rich and full and free from the curse that had held everyone else in my family back. So, in desperation, I contacted the employer from IBM that I had worked for the previous year in high school and asked him for a job. I was trained on how to fix keypunch machines, and I knew that this was something I could go back to easily. To my surprise, he had an offer for me that looked pretty good. The only stipulation was that I would have to go to Washington, D.C., and go through a training session before starting work. So, I packed my things and left school behind to pursue an early career and do what I thought was the only thing I could. But when I arrived in Washington, something in my soul kept tugging on me and pulling me back. It was a yearning that I could not explain, and in a lot of ways, I could hear the voice of my grandmother inside of me, urging me to go back to school. It was at that moment that I realized that if I had stayed where I was, I would be an hourly employee for the rest of my life, thus putting me in a place that I said I would never be. The urge was strong enough on the inside for me to quit the training program, pack up my bags, and get on a Greyhound bus through Chicago to get back to Indiana and re-enroll in school. School was starting in two weeks and I hadn't registered for any classes, so I had to throw myself on the mercy of the registrar and pray for a miracle. God was listening — not only did the registrar let me back in, on probation, she gave me a job in the registrar's office (to keep an eye on me ... I think). I persevered and ended up graduating three years later with a Bachelor of Social Work degree.

Pride and Prejudice

"Don't believe everything you hear."

When I read the prejudicial rumors in the paper and heard about them on television — that the French and the German people, supposedly, did not want any American soldiers in their country — I was saddened and infuriated. I hate racism of any kind. The news said that they didn't want us in their country because they were opposed to the war, but hadn't the Germans welcomed us years ago when we came to set them free from the tyrannical rule of Hitler. I thought, "Didn't the Iraqi people deserve freedom, too?" I didn't mind being a soldier, but I didn't want to be a pawn in another racial fight that would attach itself to my memory.

As a middle-aged African-American female, I've had my share of racial incidents. I have been called the "N" word on several occasions, but never as much as when I was a poor, struggling undergraduate at Valparaiso University. It must have been spring or fall, because there was no snow on the ground and I can faintly remember smelling the cherry blossoms of the trees from the tundra on north campus. It was the early '80s and the school for some unknown reason had been the target of pranks by local racists. The "crazies" had been trying to intimidate the minority-student population into leaving the school. There were only about 50 black students, out of a student body of 1200. We were a close-knit family and always tried to help each other out.

"Valpo" was nestled away in a quaint bedroom community of mostly middle-class whites who took the train into Chicago to work, owned their own small business in town, or worked for the university. It was the classic storybook, small, privileged college town. The town square was beautifully lined with trees, shrubs and small variety stores all around. Valpo's claim to fame was that it was the hometown of Orville Redenbacher, the gourmet-popcorn man. Outside, "Valpo" looked picture-perfect, but in the surrounding communities, something insidious was brewing.

During my sophomore year, I got a peak at the hidden volcano. For close to a week, some crazy locals had been driving around campus yelling racial obscenities and taunting black students. They had even tried to burn a cross on the hill of the school's Chapel of Resurrection. After several confirmed incidents, the school wisely became alarmed and offered to tighten security by having the entire black-student population move into one dorm. Some of the black students' parents caught wind of what was going on and immediately began un-enrolling their children. I had no money and no place to go, so like others, I chose to stick it out and prayed that the storm of racism would pass. We were told by the administration to go every place we needed in twos, for protection — to classes, work, sorority meetings, etc.

Although we carefully followed the instructions of the administration, the inevitable still happened. My friend Reggie and I were strolling up from the south of campus together late one Sunday afternoon, having a conversation and enjoying the weather. While strolling along, we were caught off guard when almost run over by two angry-looking, young white boys driving a dark-colored, late-model '60s Chevy Impala. They spotted us walking and began yelling the "N" word at us, louder and louder. In an instant, they spun their car around, sped up, and began chasing us through the parking lot. Reggie told me to run in and out between the cars until I could make my way up to the Student Union building for help. He stayed in the parking lot, using his body as a decoy until the police could come for help. Maybe Reggie thought that by doing this, we could catch these crazies once and for all. I remember falling down and getting back up as I ran up the backside of the hill toward safety. I was scared, but quietly praying. I had been in fights before, but I never had to run for my life. This was worse than a fight, because their weapon of choice was a car, which would've been lethal. As I tried to catch my breath at the Student Union, I was shaking. Wasn't I at a Christian school? Hadn't I left the ghetto and violence behind for a chance at the good life at a school full of promises? I shook my head in despair, and began to tell everyone around what was happening and to go and rescue Reggie. When we all got back down to the parking lot, the crazies had already driven away. Reggie was still there — OK. I guess they'd had enough Sunday-afternoon fun, using us as human targets. Coming close to being run over is something that you remember all your life, particularly when it is because of the color of your skin. I will never forget that day. That day was just as remarkable as the day the German soldiers first illustrated to us what they were really made of.

Every morning, the Chaplain staff was asked to write short devotions to send out on the Internet, to those who wanted some kind of spiritual motivation to help make it through their long, arduous days. One of my favorite devotions came from a chaplain's wife.

She was a schoolteacher or a staff person working for the Department of Defense schools at Ramstein Air Base. Ramstein was about six miles down the mountain from Landstuhl. One morning, while running late for work, she had to wait over 30 minutes to get on base. Needless to say, she was agitated and fuming under her breath — like most of us are when running late. As she sat in her hot car, she surveyed the long line and began to wonder out loud if the German guards were "sleeping" on duty. But, as she crept closer, a rare scene began to unfold before her eyes.

The line for security checks wasn't just moving slowly, it had been temporarily shut down. Instead of being manned by at least 10 German soldiers, it was being staffed by one. All of the other German soldiers had left their post; they were standing in line facing the road, 50 meters away from the entrance to the gate, at the position of attention — saluting. Their heads and eyes were straight across the horizon; their arms were bent at the required 90-degree angle; and their fingers were barely touching their brows, but there was no flag, no music and no parade. It seemed eerie; they were just standing still and saluting.

She wondered to herself what was going on, when suddenly, she saw about three fully loaded blue rescue Air Force buses, with big red crosses on them, speeding for the exit. They were carrying wounded American soldiers. The war was young still, but it had quickly become the custom of these German soldiers to honor the wounded American troops, whenever they passed through their gate, by saluting them and making everyone wait to provide a quick exit pathway to the hospital.

The German soldiers not only honored our wounded troops, they also supplied specialty doctors, such as neurologists, when we were short on staff. When we needed dialysis machines, the hospital at the University in Homburg would allow us to send over soldiers for treatments. There would be times when the German doctors on call arrived before the Air Force buses or ambulances. I never once heard the doctors complain; they just stood by and waited patiently for the opportunity to serve.

The post had two Fisher Houses (like Ronald McDonald houses), where approximately 16 family members could stay, but no more. The houses were beautifully equipped with guest rooms and common-living areas to watch TV, play games and do laundry, as well as a kitchen to cook a small gourmet meal, if desired. Unfortunately, as the war intensified, both of the houses were always full. In response to this problem, the local Germans from Landstuhl offered us hotel rooms in one of their best establishments, at cost, to help accommodate some of the family members who had no other place to stay.

The people from Germany that I encountered wanted desperately to help us and the wounded soldiers. They didn't want to be viewed in a negative way anymore than we did. Pride has a terrible way of turning things ugly, and unlike in the reports we had heard from all of the media, they were not prejudice against us individually. It was just a lack of understanding. You can't always believe the hype — people need people, regardless of race, nationality or ethnicity. I, for one, am glad that I had the opportunity to see firsthand the kindness, dignity and respect the Germans displayed for our wounded troops and their family members. I know prejudice or hatred when I see it, and I never encountered any of that from the Germans. The German soldiers understood something very important — sacrifice without gain, and service for freedom. They knew what it meant to fight and be seriously injured for your country. I only saw people who were willing to help other people in need, even if they didn't agree with the reason we were there. The German soldiers showed respect for our fallen troops the best way they could, a small but significant gesture toward understanding for both countries.

The Jar

"What matters most is the inside."

Early along, I knew in my heart that this deployment was not an accident, but an act of God. I was intended to be here. Make no mistake about it — God had written my name down in the book of life with a big star next to "Operation Iraqi Freedom." He had an extraordinary work for me to do for others and a long-overdue work He needed done in me. All throughout this book, I have talked about the lessons I learned from serving others, but right in the middle of the war, God taught me an incredible lesson about life and myself.

The command leadership at LRMC had commissioned three local trainers to become certified in teaching "The 7 Habits of Highly Effective People," by Stephen Covey. It was the commander's desire that every leader in the hospital attend a three-day course on-site. So when I was told that I had to take off three days from work to go to this training program, I almost lost it. I thought, "What is going on here? They take me thousands of miles away from home, stick me in a dive to live in, make me into a modern-day Father Mulcahy, and now tell me to stop all I was doing to go sit in a classroom and learn about leadership for three days." I just knew that the commander and his staff had lost their minds. I didn't come to train; it was too late for that. I came to work and to minister to wounded, hurting, and dying troops.

Needless to say, I was so upset that I had to sign up twice for the training class. I wiggled my way out of the first session; naturally, I convinced myself I was just too busy. And just when I thought I had escaped going to the training altogether, my boss identified me in a meeting as being delinquent and strongly encouraged me to sign up again, ASAP. Being a good soldier, I signed up immediately. I figured that, at best, I would get three days off of bus detail and maybe get some real rest, as the class was from 7:30 a.m. to 4:30 p.m. daily, with no overtime and no weekend work.

I remember the first day of class like it was yesterday. They asked all of us to introduce ourselves, and state why we were there and what we hoped to get out of the class. I raised my hand swiftly and said very candidly, without hesitation, that I was ordered and figured that at least I could get some rest. I was caustic and admitted that I had been to leadership-training classes like this before, at Pepsi, Kraft and Wal-Mart, where everyone went in smiling, was motivated for a while, but where, ultimately, things didn't changed at the core.

Day two, I would be changed for the rest of my life. During a lesson on "Putting First Things First," we were viewing a videotape in which the leader asked the audience how they could get everything that was on a table (rocks, sand and pebbles) into a medium-sized fish jar with a small opening. The leader guaranteed it could be done. He said that the jar represented our lives. The rocks represented the important things in our lives. And finally, the sand and pebbles represented the little things in our lives. Being a visual learner, I immediately thought no one could fit everything into that jar. The leader called on student after student in the tape to try, and every one of them failed.

Finally, he demonstrated that to get everything into the jar you had to put the biggest objects (i.e., rocks) in first and then fill it up with whatever was left. Otherwise, your jar would always be filled up first with the little things, leaving the biggest ones out.

There was a silent hush in the room on the video. He continued, saying that most of us make decisions on a daily basis where we fail to consider first the things that matter most to us; and that if we wanted success in our lives or careers, we would have to learn, as leaders, to make all of our decisions based first on the most-important things in our lives.

As what he said marinated in my head and my heart, tears began to well up inside of me. The proverbial light bulb went off, and I realized why I had been losing my own struggle for so long. I had been going around majoring in the minors, and using my time and energy on the trivial instead of the significant. Ever since I left college, I thought that the most important thing was chasing the all-mighty dollar at any cost, as long as it was legal. I had left the Army for the Pepsi Cola Company, and Pepsi for Kraft, and Kraft for Wal-Mart — but not because I was dissatisfied with the work, because the work was just a performance and had nothing to do with me and everything to do with the money. Sitting in the class, I finally wanted to know about me. I wanted to know what mattered when the money was stripped away. I wanted to know what was in me. All of a sudden, I was numb, cold and in shock. I didn't know my heart. I didn't know what was inside, and I couldn't articulate what my "rocks" really were. I could lie and be convincing, but at 43, I felt like a blank sheet of paper.

I vowed that day not to go to sleep until I could honestly identify what mattered besides the money. This wasn't exactly the assignment that I was given, but it was the one I needed to do. Figuring out what mattered most would not be easy. First, I would have to be honest and deal with myself. Second, I would have to tell and accept the truth of the stories of my life, and value them for what they were trying to show me. And lastly, I would have to be willing to manage whatever it was, and ultimately, to do something about it. It was a scary proposition. But I wanted to meet the big rocks. I wanted to know what was most important. I wanted to see into the recesses of my soul and become comfortable in my own skin. I came to war physically, mentally and spiritually exhausted, and tired of living my life the same old way. After all, I had prayed for clarity, change and answers because I was going through the motions in my job, in my house, and even with those I loved. I was on autopilot, and things and people just didn't mean the same to me anymore. I hated it. Daily, I was struggling for meaning. How uncanny that God would separate me from the things I cherished most and send me to this war, knowing that this obstacle awaited me.

As I thought about the truth, I realized that I had been in a situation like this before. I was 29 and had just been diagnosed with 28 tumors, mostly fibroids, in my uterus and two polyps. It all happened so suddenly. I was living my life as a single, black career woman in Evansville, Indiana, when I passed out in my home on my way to work. I came to and realized that I had been out most of the day. I didn't panic, but I was scared. I called a doctor and she suggested that I come in right away. I called work, telling them I was sick and would be out a few days. The next day, after a trying extremely hard to find a doctor I could see on one days notice. I found one who ordered an ultrasound of my uterus, and within hours, told me that I would be on my way to surgery to have an exploratory procedure to try and save my uterus that was now full with over 40 tumors. After I picked myself up off the floor, I called my mom and my family, and they all rearranged their lives to come to the surgery in two days. On the day of the surgery, I remember my three nieces, ages 7, 5 and 2, sitting on my chest, saying how much they "wuved" me. I remember lying on that gurney, wondering about my life, wondering what mattered most. I remember saying that it was those around me and those I loved. Not the money, the job or the new condo.

Truth isn't truth until you set it free. And in that little bedroom in Germany, I was set free. I'd had the truth since I was 29, but somewhere along the way, I stopped believing it. I started adding too many pebbles and too much sand into my jar. Clearly, I knew what mattered most, and it wasn't the high five-figure salary, the big cars or fancy clothes, but those whom I had birthed, those whom I have nurtured, and those who have nurtured me. It wasn't as hard as I thought. The truth is always closer than you think.

Saying Goodbye

"How do I say goodbye?"

Everybody wanted to go home. We were tired, and we'd had our dreams dashed once before, so we were very cautious when we heard rumors that we would be leaving by late February or early March. We heard that another hospital unit from California had been identified. But I don't think anybody really started cheering until we saw "the whites of their eyes" — that is, the eyes of the replacement-unit members, as they were touring the facility in Germany.

About two weeks before our departure, we were briefed about leaving. They told us which groups we would travel in, what days we would fly, what we were to wear, where we would go to demobilize, and what gear we were allowed to take back. Having lived for an entire year in makeshift apartments, most of us had accumulated a lot of personal items.

First, we had to decide what to do with the items that had been collected over the past months. By this time, we had completely stocked our kitchen with pots, pans, a coffee machine, knives, dishes, tablecloths, and lots of other necessary items. Before it was all over, our apartment had been equipped with televisions, books, towels, shower curtains, civilian clothes, and many personal items. We decided as a group that all of the "apartment stuff" that was personally purchased from thrift stores and retrieved from the curb on "junk days," we would leave for the new crew. We remembered what it was like to enter a stark, barren three-bedroom apartment with eight beds, two couches, a couple of tables and chairs. We had all been accustomed to so much more, and it had taken a deep emotional toll on us when we first arrived. It wasn't a tent, but it wasn't exactly home either.

Anything that did not fit into our two duffel bags and personal carry-on had to be mailed back to the States at our own expense. To accomplish this arduous task, we had to stand in long mail lines. I can imagine that some folks suddenly acquired some short-term packing skills as they tried to fit all that they could into their duffel bags. I think I fell into the "moderately junkie" category and spent close to $400 shipping extra clothes, books and souvenirs home.

As the day for us to leave grew closer, we had to out-process through the hospital. We had to go back through every department, get a check mark, and swear that we were physically and mentally well enough to travel. We looked like young kids who had been let loose at an Easter-egg hunt. Surprisingly, there were those who had been ill or had surgery during the deployment, and though they were now well, they were still scrutinized with a fine-tooth comb. Those who failed the screening were placed on medical hold, which meant that they had to wait longer before they could leave. Their hearts were saddened beyond belief when they were told that they could leave Germany but not the Army until approximately 30–45 days later, after further medical screening.

We were divided into two separate flight groups on two different days, which was decided by lottery so everyone would have a chance at a first flight. I was in the first group — praise the Lord. At first, I felt guilty and even offered my seat to others, but they all graciously declined. Our flight home, on a chartered plane, took us through Ireland; Bangor, Maine; and then finally, to an Air Force base in San Antonio,

Texas. We were glad to be back on American soil, even though we were sad to leave one another.

Boarding the plane to leave was a very intense, emotional moment for me. It was the first time that I had broken down in front of my soldiers, and I was near tears as I climbed the stairs to the airplane. After spending a rough year together, the bonds that were formed were stronger than ever.

We were kept in a staging area that was an empty warehouse with hundreds of bunks inside. There was a phone area, a couple of Internet hookups, some water and candy. At first, we didn't know how long we would stay there, but fortunately, we only stayed a couple of hours.

Even though I had never heard of it before, Ambassador Air, our charter airline, felt like first class on Lufthansa. At that moment, it was the best airline in the world. We flew from Germany to Ireland, where we made a fuel stop. The air was thick and a bit chilly, and the airport was old, but the people were warm and gracious. When we arrived, they had plenty of food available, as well as tall glasses of dark-brown Irish beer, phones, and candy full of liquor. We only stayed for about an hour before preparing to go on home. We returned to the

States through Bangor, Maine, which was our customs entry point. The last time we flew out of Bangor, late at night on the eve of March 19, it had been a solemn time. This time was a little different — we arrived full of joy, quietly expecting a big heroes' welcome home. It wasn't big, but it was sincere, as old war vets, and their spouses and friends, lined the corridor to shake our hands and say, "Welcome home." I think the most striking thing I remember about coming back through Bangor was that the people were handing out cell phones encouraging us to make calls home for free. It turned out that a cell-phone company in town had made provisions for us to use the cell phones to call anybody, anywhere, on American soil; just to say we had made it back. Another thing that will always stand out in my memory is coming down the tunnel, away from the plane, seeing the names and pictures of all the fallen heroes from the war on the walls. Some names and faces we recognized as those we had treated in the hospital and had lost, and some we did not recognize, but we honored them as heroes just the same. Being in that tunnel 12 months later was a stark reminder that everyone who left out through Bangor didn't make it back.

The people in Bangor were *WONDERFUL,* just simply wonderful; they made our journey back home one that I will always remember. After a two hour layover, we left Bangor en route to Fort Sam Houston in San Antonio. As a hospital unit, we were fortunate enough to be mobilized and de-mobilized through the Army's Medical Command post and not through Fort Hood, Texas, where thousands of troops were being processed in and out daily, like cattle.

We arrived very late at the military airport, and unfortunately for us, only a few buses and ground crew members were still waiting. There was no big band or banner or spouses club to sing our praises, just a handful of old, true GS-civilian employees. It was late, and even though we were alone, we had the task of physically off-loading our own bags from underneath the plane. We also had to stack them under the civilian Greyhound-looking buses that would take us back to *our* housing at Fort Sam Houston. At this point, honestly, even *I* was discouraged, but I was also hopeful, knowing that in 3–5 days we would all be home. Our housing turned out to be an old, four-story, dilapidated training barracks that had been slated for renovation. When I saw this poor contrivance of a housing unit, the wind was knocked out of my sails.

We had endured enough, been through hell and back, only to be brought back to substandard housing. We were issued linens, and as we climbed the stairs of our building, we found small, mildew-smelling rooms with bunks and bathrooms that needed a deep cleaning. We were tired and in need of showers, so we dug around to find some cleaning supplies to clean the bathrooms *before* we would use them. I slept on my bunk that night with my uniform on, and I was determined to find better accommodations first thing the next day. For the first time, the small amount of positive motivation that I had was lost. All we wanted was a decent place to sleep, and even that was out of our reach at this point.

Some people in my unit were from San Antonio, or close by, so they were allowed to go home as long as they were back by the 0530 formation to start out-processing. Outside our barracks, there were a handful of happy, teary-eyed family members waiting patiently for their soldiers to be released. It was great for some of them, but 90 percent of us still had miles to go — to Little Rock, Arkansas; Shreveport, Louisiana; Dallas, Texas; or other points, south or west — before we would be home.

Having been to Fort Sam Houston before, I knew how to get around a little bit, and one valuable piece of information that I had not forgotten was where the rental-car office was. So as soon as I could, on day two after my first long break, I made a beeline over to the Enterprise Rental Car counter to pick up any car they had available. I figured I'd use the car to get myself back and forth from out-processing appointments; I'd find a decent hotel and help shuttle other soldiers where they needed to go, including the airport, if needed.

We had morning briefings, and we were given a schedule of where to go and when, but we were pretty much on our own to get to our appointed place of duty on time. We had appointments for medical, dental, personal records, awards, shots, finance and travel. Most places were within a 2-mile radius, so a lot of people just walked around in the heat to get where they needed to go. It was March, and we had just come from 20-degree weather to 60-degree weather. When I arrived at Enterprise, almost every car was already gone. I ended up with a large vehicle and was as happy as I could be to have some control of my life back. To treat myself, I made a reservation for a king-sized bed at the Westin Riverwalk and thought to myself, "Look out, heavenly bed, here I come!" Being a major, I had the money to get a nice room and a car. Most enlisted soldiers could not and had to endure their stale, meager accommodations for 2–3 more days. That's one reason I acted like a taxi-service, all day and all night, when the need arose.

I will always remember walking into the Westin River Walk in uniform late the second night. The doorman asked if I needed help; he was the first civilian, nonmilitary-type person to say "Thank you" to me for my service. The female attendant at the counter smiled and even gave me a room with a nice view — and of course, the military discount. I was in heaven! I still had to make formation at 0530, but just knowing that I had a beautiful place to sleep now renewed my confidence and restored my attitude. This small thing made all the difference for me. I had taken care of so many others; I took pride in doing a job well-done for more than 12 months — but now, I was going to take care of myself and get a little TLC. It almost felt sinful.

I became "Shuttle" Hopkins, as I ended up dropping off about 10–15 folks at the airport the last two days. It is hard to say goodbye, and as I saw soldier after soldier leave, I finally knew what those "ole" vets felt for their "ole" war buddies. I understood now why tears come quickly to their eyes when they reach back and recount their times together. Twelve months ago, I didn't know a soul; I didn't know anyone's name or family or story. Now, I felt like I was saying goodbye to an older sister or a younger brother who I knew in my heart that I would not see again. It was hard to care for wounded soldiers who over time whom I got to know well. It was extremely difficult saying a prayer over those who paid the ultimate price. Every single time a soldier was dropped off; everybody got teary eyed, cried, and held hands, and promised to stay in touch. It was a defining moment — a bittersweet ending to a yearlong deployment.

The last goodbye was the most difficult for me though, as I had to let go of a chaplain's greatest asset (other than her Bible) — her chaplain assistant. Mine was a gem. He was a blessing from above who protected, encouraged, trained, sheltered and motivated me daily. He worked beside me for the whole year rarely complaining and always smiling. Jerry had become more than someone I worked with, he felt like my little brother. He was the last person I would say goodbye to at the airport. I let him out of the car and gave him a big, warm hug. I asked him to call me when he got home safe. It was almost like I would see him again, but I knew better. I hopped back into my car and pulled away from the curb, as I turned to see if Jerry was still standing there, and tears began to flood out of me. Was it really over? Was this the end? Wasn't this how it started for me 12 months before, crying all alone in my car? Suddenly, I realized I had come full circle in this deployment. I was halfway home and back again.

Epilogue

I am back in America now a few years removed from the war as I sit and write this. Physically, I am thousands of miles away, and hundreds of days have passed since living daily in an environment of constant trauma. Everyday I see and hear things that remind me of my service – buses, planes, hospitals, and soldiers. The war is never far from me. I have had the privilege of talking and listening to hundreds of veterans and active duty soldiers since my return and I know that the war is not far from them either. Some still cry, some walk with a limp, some are just silent or violent. My youngest son, Adam still asks me periodically, when I am packing a suitcase if I am going back to Germany. My oldest son, Samuel sings a remarkable lullaby, that he made up to comfort his brother" Don't cry mommy will be here tomorrow" just enough to remind me that they both still carry their own battle scars.

War affects everyone who goes and those loved ones who stay behind. As a chaplain, it is my prayer that as a nation we will find a way out of this war and a way to heal our land, our families, our government and ourselves. If you are one of the precious few who stayed behind and loved a soldier from afar, I applaud you. I ask that you be patient with us because "God and the war are not finished with us yet." If you are a soldier who served, I ask you to remember that your loved ones did not serve and they are not the enemy. They may have sympathy, but empathy is beyond them at that point. Love them through this difficult time, and talk to them lovingly, as much as possible. You can have a wonderful future, but it will take everyone concerned.

Because I am a woman of faith, I believe in the power of God and that everything is for a reason or a season. I believe that if you "hold on" long enough and trust God that He will heal your body, your mind and your soul. I also believe that between every mountain top there are many valley lows, so keep the faith. Everyday that we live and move and have our being in Him is a day closer to healing. God is working it out for me and I am praying daily that he is working it out for you too. Be encouraged my friends.

About the Author

Originally hailing from Buffalo, New York, Reverend Felicia P Hopkins received her undergraduate degree in social work from Valparaiso University. Felicia went on to obtain her Master's of Divinity from Austin Presbyterian Theological Seminary in 1996. She is now serving as the Preaching Pastor at St. Mark's United Methodist Church in El Paso, Texas. Felicia was deployed in support of Operation Iraqi Freedom, where she served as trauma Chaplain (Major) in the U.S. Army for wounded troops, and their family members, arriving in Germany from battle in Iraq and Afghanistan. During her deployment, she humbly served more than 12,000 wounded troops.

As an inspirational speaker, Felicia Hopkins is an influential mouthpiece who motivates her audience to action by drawing from personal experience and shared wisdom to craft and deliver life-changing messages. Her inner strength and energetic persona have an undeniably infectious effect on those she encounters. Her ability to effectively communicate essential principles is a product of her never-ending thirst for knowledge. Felicia travels all over the nation as an inspirational speaker to various groups.

www.feliciahopkins.org

CPSIA information can be obtained at www.ICGtesting.com
Printed in the USA
LVOW05s0114190913

353065LV00001B/10/P